Collins

DISCOVER GEOGRAPHY

Workbook 7

Mark Enser, Rebecca Kitchen,
Alan Parkinson and Robbie Woodburn
Series edited by Mark Enser

William Collins' dream of knowledge for all began with the publication of his first book in 1819.

A self-educated mill worker, he not only enriched millions of lives, but also founded a flourishing publishing house. Today, staying true to this spirit, Collins books are packed with inspiration, innovation and practical expertise.

They place you at the centre of a world of possibility and give you exactly what you need to explore it.

Published by Collins

An imprint of HarperCollins*Publishers*
The News Building, 1 London Bridge Street, London, SE1 9GF, UK

HarperCollins*Publishers*
Macken House, 39/40 Mayor Street Upper, Dublin 1, D01 C9W8, Ireland

Browse the complete Collins catalogue at collins.co.uk

© HarperCollins*Publishers* Limited 2026

10 9 8 7 6 5 4 3 2 1

A catalogue record for this publication is available from the British Library.

ISBN 978-0-00-878323-5

All rights reserved. No part of this publication may be reproduced, stored in a retrieval system, or transmitted in any form or by any means, electronic, mechanical, photocopying, recording or otherwise, without the prior written permission of the Publisher or a licence permitting restricted copying in the United Kingdom issued by the Copyright Licensing Agency Ltd, 5th Floor, Shackleton House, 4 Battle Bridge Lane, London SE1 2HX.

Without limiting the exclusive rights of any author, contributor or the publisher of this publication, any unauthorised use of this publication to train generative artificial intelligence (AI) technologies is expressly prohibited. HarperCollins also exercise their rights under Article 4(3) of the Digital Single Market Directive 2019/790 and expressly reserve this publication from the text and data mining exception.

Authors: Mark Enser, Rebecca Kitchen, Alan Parkinson and Robbie Woodburn
Publishers: Cathy Martin and Katie Sergeant
Product manager: Saaleh Patel
Project manager: Just Content
Development editor: Jo Kemp
Copyeditor: Jan Schubert
Proofreader: Rebecca Ramsden
Cover designer: Amparo Kneath, Kneath Associates
Internal designer: Steve Evans, Planet Life Art
Illustrator: Six Red Marbles

Cartography: Gordon MacGilp
Typesetter: Six Red Marbles
Production controller: Alhady Ali
Printed and bound by: Martins the Printers

Acknowledgements
The publishers gratefully acknowledge the permission granted to reproduce the copyright material in this book. Every effort has been made to trace copyright holders and to obtain their permission for the use of copyright material. The publishers will gladly receive any information enabling them to rectify any error or omission at the first opportunity.

Images

Front cover Rich Carey/Shutterstock, p2t udaya fire/Shutterstock, p21l fireFX/Shutterstock, p21c hallojulie/Shutterstock, p21r Olga Ilina/Shutterstock, p33 Designua/Shutterstock, p37 faridabegum ID 2093746/Shutterstock, p45 Betelgeusee/Shutterstock, p51 Lubo Ivanko/Shutterstock, p67 Photoongraphy/Shutterstock, p77 Mike Workman/Shutterstock, p80 Ekateryna Zubal/Shutterstock.

Textual
We are grateful to the following for permission to reproduce copyright material:

p.9 – Figure 1.4 Changes in global average temperature over the last 450,000 years. Taken from: Glacial-interglacial cycles over the past 450,000 years. Produced by Noaa – National Centers for Environmental Information. Attribution 4.0 International CC BY 4.0 Deed. p.10 – Figure 1.5 Temperature projections for the future based on emissions. Produced by GlobalChange.gov. Attribution 4.0 International CC BY 4.0 Deed. p.57 – Figure 4.4 Climate graph for Utqiagvik, Alaska produced by Climates to Travel – © climatestotravel.com. p.61 – Figure 4.5 Map showing population density in Russia. Found in Wiki Commons – File: Federal subjects of Russia by population dencity.svg. Creator has put this work in the public domain. p.78 – Table 5.2 Number of emergency food parcels distributed by food banks in the Trussell Community. © Trussell. p.82 – Figure 5.8 Percentage of food calories lost and wasted during the production process. From: World Resources Institute (WRI) and WRAP. 2015. Reducing Food Loss and Waste: Setting a Global Action Agenda. Washington, DC: World Resources Institute. Licensed under Creative Commons Attribution 4.0 (wri.org).

Contents

Introduction   iv

Chapter 1   Why does climate change?   1

Chapter 2   How might climate change affect drainage basins?   17

Chapter 3   Why does the Lake District look different from the Himalayas?   33

Chapter 4   How does life adapt to its environment   49

Chapter 5   What can be done to ensure everyone has enough food?   65

Chapter 6   What impacts will a changing climate have?   83

Introduction

Welcome to the Collins Discover Geography 7 Workbook.

This book is your place to explore ideas, practice geographical skills and record your learning as you work through the Discover Geography 7 Student's Book.

Geography is about asking questions about the world around us – why places are as they are, how they change, and how people and environments are connected. The activities in this Workbook are designed to help you think like a geographer. You will have chances to describe patterns, explain processes, interpret data and make decisions about real-world issues.

Each section of the Workbook links directly to the lessons in your Student's Book. Use it to:

- **test your understanding** after reading or discussing new ideas in class
- **practice geographical skills** such as drawing and interpreting maps, graphs and diagrams
- **apply your knowledge** to examples from different parts of the world
- **reflect on your learning** by explaining what you have found out and what questions you still have.

The Workbook also gives you space to record your own thoughts and examples, helping you build a personal record of your geographical learning. You can look back on this later to see how your understanding has developed over time.

You do not need to write long answers every time – clear explanations, labelled diagrams and short notes are all valuable ways to show what you know. Try to keep your responses neat and well-organised so that they become a useful reference for revision.

Most importantly, use this Workbook to stay curious. Geography is not just about places on a map – it is about people, patterns and possibilities. Each task is an opportunity to discover more about how our world works and to think about your role in shaping its future.

Chapter 1   Why does climate change?

1.1   What is climate?

Connect back

1 What is the difference between weather and climate?

....

....

....

2 Describe the climate of your location. How does it compare with Moscow and Riyadh?

....

....

....

....

Expand

3 Using an atlas, locate the hottest, coldest, wettest and driest places on Earth. State their latitude and longitude.

	Latitude	Longitude
Hottest:	....	....
Coldest:	....	....
Wettest:	....	....
Driest:	....	....

Chapter 1 Why does climate change?

1.1

4 A student goes out and measures the temperature using a thermometer (Figure 1.1). They report to their teacher that the temperature is 10 °C. Are they right? Why?

....

....

....

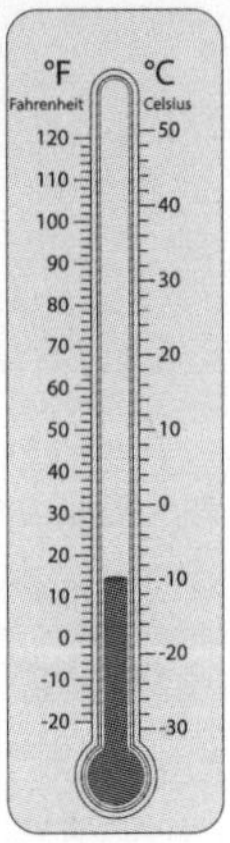

Figure 1.1

Predict

5 On the graph outline below (Figure 1.2), sketch what you think a climate graph for Antarctica might look like. Annotate your sketch to explain what you have drawn.

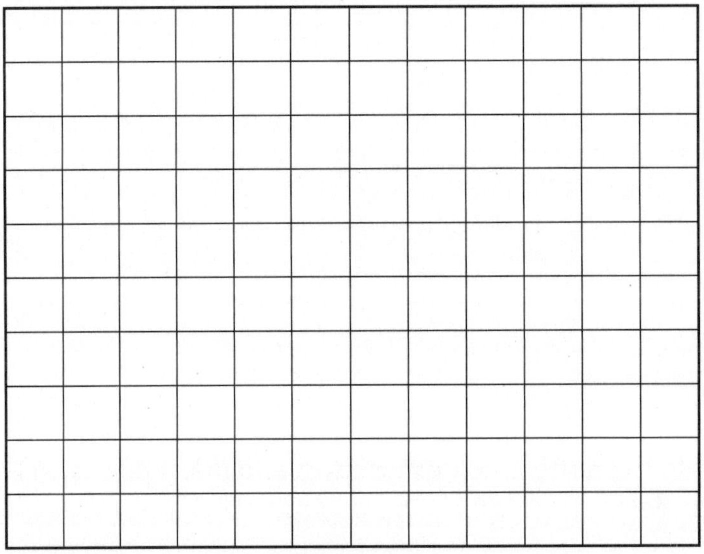

Figure 1.2

6 What challenges might living in an extreme climate – one which is very hot or very cold, very wet or very dry – bring?

....

....

....

....

....

1.2 Why is temperature different in different places?

Connect back

1 Draw a diagram to show why temperature generally changes with latitude.

2 What do we mean by 'altitude'?

....

....

Expand

3 Explain why Mount Kenya often has snow on the top of it, even though it is located close to the equator.

....

....

....

....

1.2 Chapter 1 Why does climate change?

4 Why are places near the coast cooler in summer than places inland?

....

....

....

....

Predict

5 Pick a city in an area of the world you are unfamiliar with. Use your knowledge from this lesson to try to predict what you think the temperature would be like and explain your reasoning. Then use a search engine to search for a climate graph of this city and see if you were correct.

....

....

....

....

....

....

6 What other topics that you might study in geography do you think this knowledge will be useful for? Why?

....

....

....

....

....

1.3 Why is rainfall different in different places?

Connect back

1 Draw a diagram to explain the process of relief rainfall.

2 What are the Hadley, Ferrel and polar cells?

....

....

....

Expand

3 Where would you expect to find the world's deserts? Explain why.

....

....

....

....

1.3 Chapter 1 Why does climate change?

4 Where would you expect to find the world's rainforests? Explain why.

....

....

....

....

Predict

5 Use the information from this lesson to predict and explain what the rainfall is like in your country.

....

....

....

....

....

6 Why is the information from this lesson important? What other topics might it link to?

....

....

....

....

....

1.4 How do you know what the climate is like?

Connect back

1 On a separate piece of paper, draw a spider diagram which categorises the different ways that we know what the climate is like in the past, present and future.

2 Would you like to be a meteorologist? Why?

....

....

....

Expand

3 Which type of evidence in your spider diagram do you think is most reliable? Why do you think this?

....

....

....

4 Do you think that the evidence for climate change over time is strong? Why?

....

....

....

....

Chapter 1 Why does climate change?

1.4

Predict

5 Carry out some research to find out what the climate has been like in your country over the last year, for example wetter or drier than average, early or late summer. Sketch a diagram in the space below to show what you think the tree rings would look like as a result.

6 We have evidence of climate change from places which are covered in ice (ice cores), places which have lots of trees (tree rings) and places which have ocean sediments. Are there any places where we might not have much evidence for local climate change? Mark these on the world map below (Figure 1.3) and annotate to explain your answer.

Figure 1.3 Map of the world.

1.5 How has climate changed over time?

Connect back

1 Describe the pattern of global average temperature shown in Figure 1.4.

....

....

....

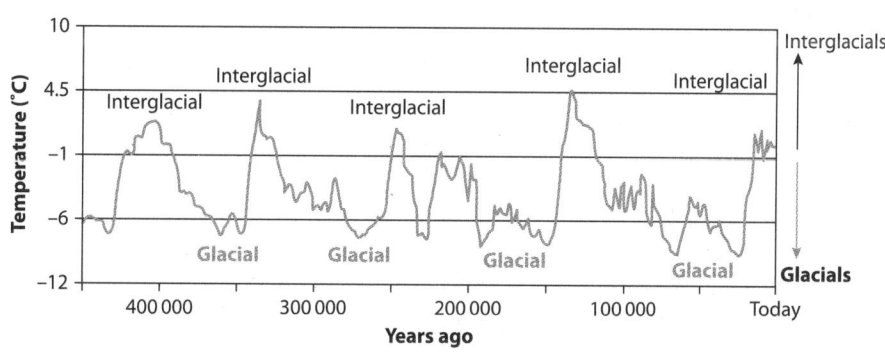

Figure 1.4 Changes in global average temperature over the last 450 000 years.

2 Do you think we are in a glacial or an interglacial now? How do you know?

....

....

....

Expand

3 Why is it important to understand the big picture of what is happening to the climate over the long term and then zoom in to look at climate data over a shorter period of time?

....

....

....

1.5 Chapter 1 Why does climate change?

4 Why do you think scientists take measurements from the pre-industrial average temperature?

....

....

Predict

5 Why do you think there is such a strong relationship between CO_2 and global average temperature?

....

....

6 Carry out some research to find out what the world might be like in each of the different scenarios shown in Figure 1.5. Add your findings to the table.

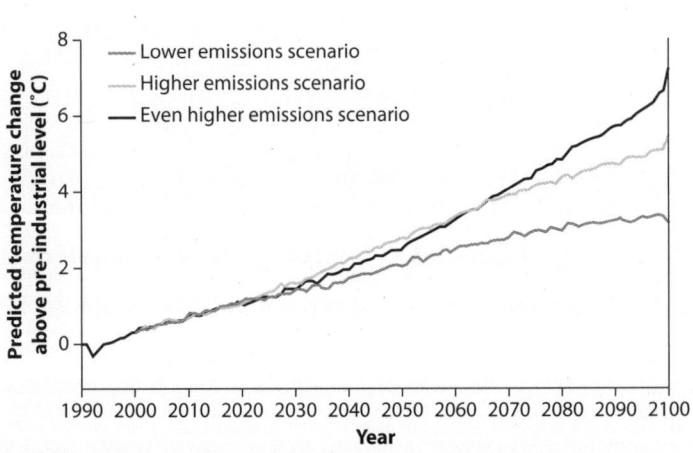

Figure 1.5 Future projections of global average temperature.

Lower emissions scenario	Higher emissions scenario	Even higher emissions scenario

10

1.6 Does climate change naturally?

Connect back

1 Write a short description of what is happening in each of the diagrams in Figure 1.6.

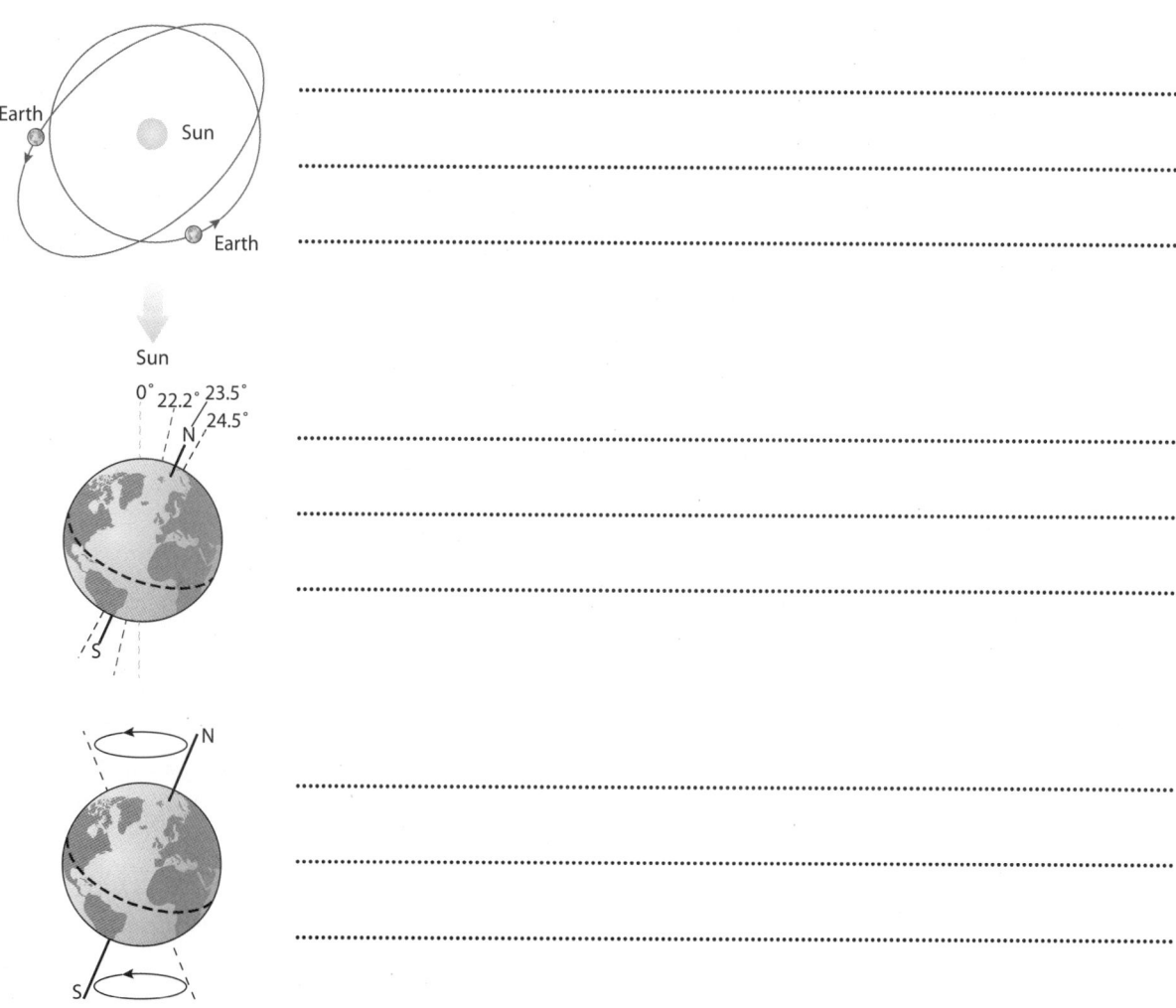

Figure 1.6 The three Milankovitch cycles of eccentricity, obliquity (tilt) and precession.

2 What is a volcanic eruption? Why do you think some volcanic eruptions are more likely to cause a change in the climate than others?

1.6 Chapter 1 Why does climate change?

Expand

3 Which of the three natural factors – Milankovitch cycles, volcanic activity or sunspot cycles – do you think has the greatest influence over changes in climate? Why do you think this?

....

....

....

4 Why do you think the Tropic of Cancer and the Tropic of Capricorn are 23½° north and south of the equator? (HINT: It is to do with one of the Milankovitch cycles.)

....

....

....

Predict

5 'We are overdue another ice age.' To what extent do you agree with this statement?

....

....

....

6 Do Milankovitch cycles just affect planet Earth? Carry out some research to see whether other planets experience similar cycles.

....

....

....

1.7 How have humans changed the climate?

Connect back

1 Draw a diagram to explain the enhanced greenhouse effect.

2 Make a list of some of the most common greenhouse gases.

....

....

3 Explain how the burning of fossil fuels has increased the concentration of greenhouse gases in the atmosphere.

....

....

....

....

1.7 Chapter 1 Why does climate change?

Expand

4 The concentrations of all the greenhouse gases in the atmosphere have increased. Why do we mainly focus on CO_2?

....

....

....

5 Carry out some research in a book or on the internet about one of the other greenhouse gases (not CO_2). State **three** things that you have learned. How does this information help you to better understand the enhanced greenhouse effect?

1 ....

2 ....

3 ....

Predict

6 Which type of human activity do you think is the most damaging in terms of climate change? Why do you think this? Suggest **three** ways in which humans could reduce their impact in this area.

1 ....

2 ....

3 ....

7 Imagine that humans continue to burn fossil fuels, cut down forests and increase livestock farming at current rates. How do you think the concentration of greenhouse gases in the atmosphere – and the Earth's climate – will change over the next 50 years?

....

....

....

1.8 Will climate change everywhere?

Connect back

1 Explain what is meant by Arctic amplification.

....
....
....
....

2 Why is melting permafrost such a problem?

....
....
....
....

Expand

3 Carry out some research in a book or on the internet to find out more about climate change in the tropics. How are places likely to be impacted? Why? Why do you think this knowledge is important?

1.8 Chapter 1 Why does climate change?

4 Look at the cross-section of some soil found in a region of permafrost in Figure 1.7. What do you think the 'active layer' is? Why is this not a good environment for building?

....

....

....

....

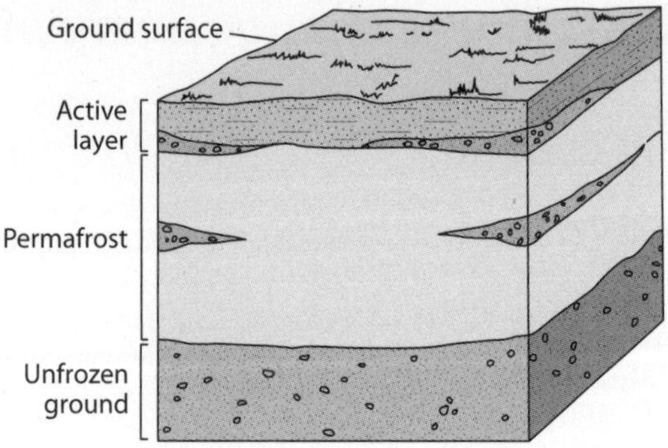

Figure 1.7 A cross-section of soil in a region of permafrost.

Predict

5 The Democratic Republic of Congo (DRC) is a country located in the tropics. Predict how climate change will affect this country. Why do you think this?

....

....

....

....

6 'The Arctic amplification only affects places near the Arctic.' To what extent do you agree with this statement?

....

....

....

....

Chapter 2: How might climate change affect drainage basins?

2.1 What are drainage basins and what is climate change?

Revisit

1 Use your knowledge of the water cycle from the Student's Book to add the labels in the correct places on the diagram below.

Labels: Evaporation, Condensation, Precipitation, Overland flow, Interception, Transpiration, Infiltration, Percolation, Through flow, Groundwater flow.

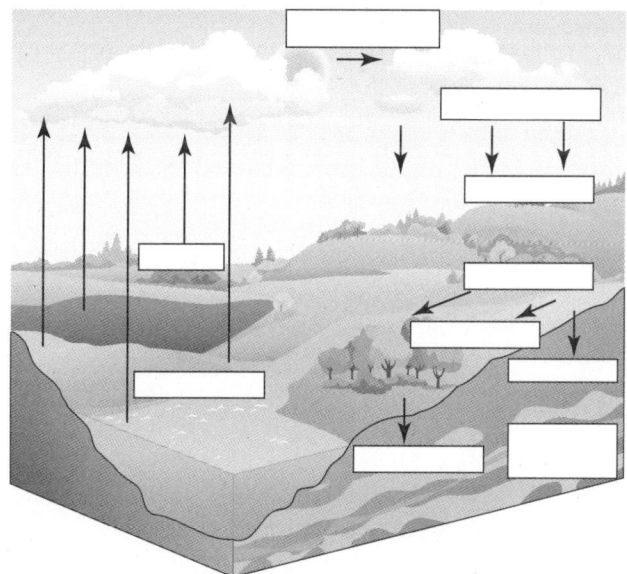

Figure 2.1 The water cycle.

2 Think about what you have learned about drainage basins. How could climate change affect the water cycle in a drainage basin?

....

....

....

3 Using your knowledge of flooding, what are **two** ways that climate change can increase the risk of floods?

1 ....

2 ....

2.1 Chapter 2 How might climate change affect drainage basins?

Expand

4 You learned that climate change can cause more intense rainfall. How might this affect plants and animals living near rivers? Give examples.

....

....

....

5 Climate change can lead to faster snowmelt. How could this impact people living in mountainous areas? Aim for **three** reasons.

1 ....

2 ....

3 ....

Predict

6 Imagine you are the mayor of a coastal city. How would you prepare your city for the possibility of more frequent flooding due to climate change?

....

....

....

....

7 If climate change continues to warm the Earth, how do you think it might change rainfall patterns in your local area in the next 50 years?

....

....

....

....

2.2 How does climate change affect water systems?

Revisit

1 Think about what you have learned about the water cycle. How might climate change alter this cycle in a drainage basin?

....

....

....

Expand

2 Use the data in Table 2.1 to create a bar chart for rainfall in the Midwest USA over the past 70 years (Figure 2.2). Write one sentence to describe the pattern.

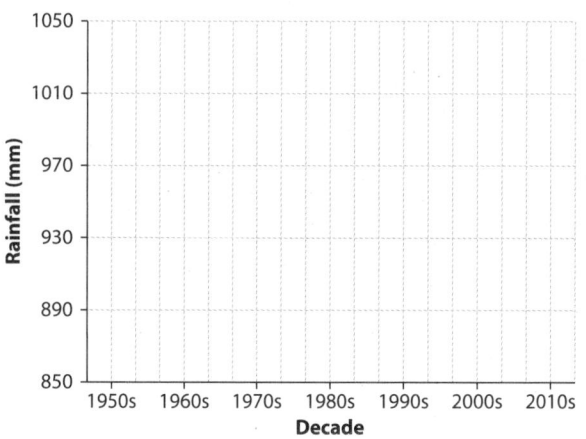

Decade	Estimated average annual rainfall (approx.)
1950s	890 mm
1960s	915 mm
1970s	965 mm
1980s	940 mm
1990s	990 mm
2000s	1015 mm
2010s	1040 mm

Figure 2.2 Approximate annual rainfall in the US Midwest, 1950s–2010s.

Table 2.1 Approximate annual rainfall in the US Midwest, 1950s–2010s.

....

....

3 Climate scientists predict more intense rainfall due to climate change. How might this affect plants and animals living near rivers? Provide **two** examples.

1 ....

2 ....

2.2 Chapter 2 How might climate change affect drainage basins?

4 Climate change can lead to faster snowmelt in mountainous regions. Explain **three** ways this could impact people living in these areas.

1 ....

2 ....

3 ....

Predict

5 Imagine you are in charge of water management for a coastal city. How would you prepare your city for the possibility of more frequent flooding due to climate change? List **three** strategies.

1 ....

2 ....

3 ....

6 Scientists suggest that climate change might alter rainfall patterns. How do you think this could affect agriculture in your local area over the next 50 years?

....

....

....

....

....

2.3 What are the causes and effects of flooding?

....

Figure 2.3 How can the type of land rain falls on impact the amount of surface run-off and the scale of flood risk?

Revisit

1 Take a look at the photographs in Figure 2.3. Think about which will cause more surface run-off. Add one of the following labels to each image:

less surface run-off   some surface run-off   lots of surface run-off

2 Think about what you have learned about drainage basins. How might the shape of a drainage basin affect the likelihood of flooding?

....

....

....

....

3 Recall what you know about precipitation. How could different types of rainfall (for example, light rain versus heavy downpour) impact flooding?

1 ....

2 ....

Expand

4 You have learned that human activities can contribute to flooding. Give **two** examples of how urban development might increase flood risk.

1 ....

2 ....

Chapter 2 How might climate change affect drainage basins?

5 Flooding can have both short-term and long-term effects. Describe **three** ways flooding might impact a community over time.

1 ....
....

2 ....
....

3 ....
....

Predict

6 Imagine you are designing a new town near a river. What **three** features would you include to reduce the risk of flooding?

1 ....
....

2 ....
....

3 ....
....

7 How do you think climate change might affect the frequency and severity of floods in your region over the next 30 years?

....
....
....
....
....

2.4 To what extent does climate change increase flood risk?

Revisit

1 Recall what you have learned about the water cycle. How might rising global temperatures affect different parts of this cycle?

....

....

....

....

2 Think about what you know about sea levels. How could rising sea levels contribute to increased flood risk in coastal areas?

....

....

3 Shade/mark all coastal regions at risk from sea-level rise and flooding.

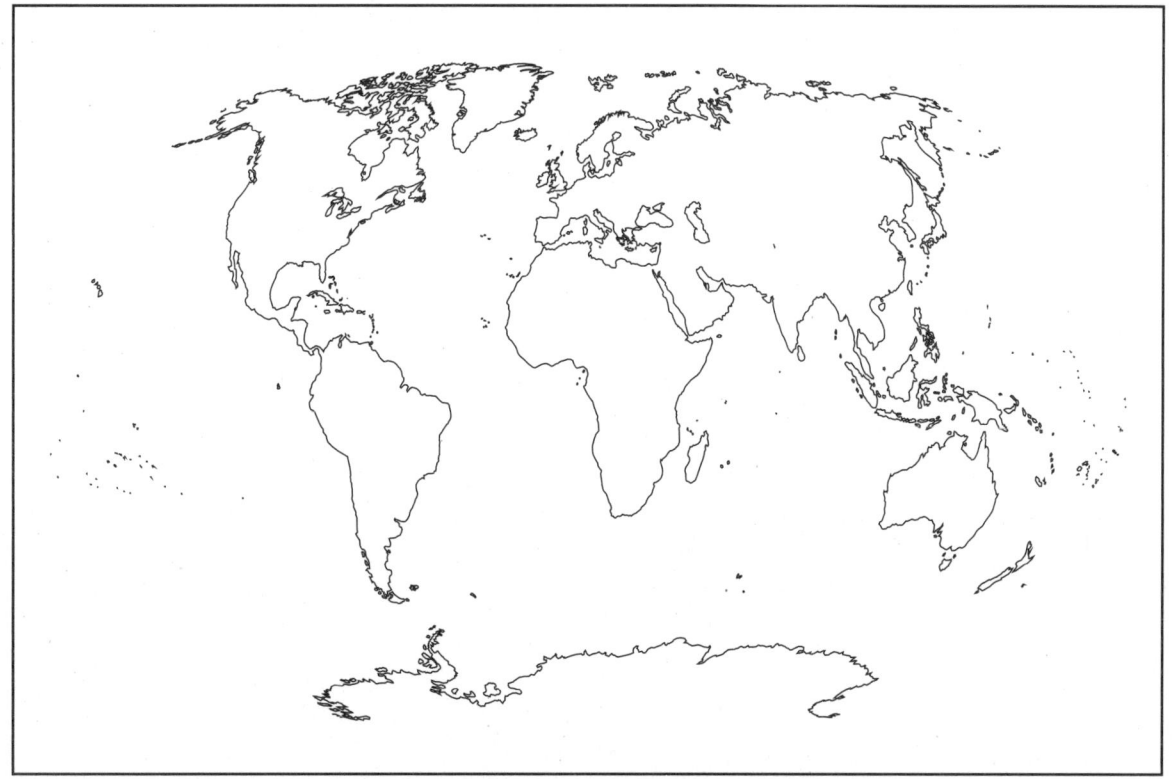

Figure 2.4 World map.

2.4 Chapter 2 How might climate change affect drainage basins?

Expand

4 Climate change can lead to more extreme weather events. Explain how this might affect the intensity and frequency of floods.

....

....

....

5 Describe **three** ways that melting glaciers due to climate change could impact flood risk in different parts of the world.

1 ....

2 ....

3 ....

Predict

6 Imagine you are a city planner in a flood-prone area. What **three** strategies would you implement to prepare for increased flood risk due to climate change?

1 ....

2 ....

3 ....

7 How do you think increased flood risk from climate change might affect global migration patterns in the next 50 years?

....

....

....

....

....

2.5 What are the causes and effects of drought?

Revisit

1 Think about what you have learned about the water cycle. How might changes in precipitation patterns lead to drought?

....

....

2 Recall what you know about climate zones. How might the location of a region affect its susceptibility to drought?

....

....

Expand

3 Using your knowledge of the effects of droughts, add the following descriptions to either the primary effects column or the secondary effects column in Table 2.2.

> Farmers are worried   Food costs more
> People move from farming areas into towns and cities   Soil becomes worse
> Not enough food or water for animals   Farmers lose money   Wildfires occur
> Habitats are destroyed   Crops die   Demand for farming equipment decreases
> Water levels in dams and reservoirs go down

Primary effects	Secondary effects

Table 2.2 The effects of drought.

Chapter 2 How might climate change affect drainage basins?

4 You have learned that droughts can have various effects on the environment. Describe **two** ways drought might impact wildlife in an ecosystem.

1 ....

2 ....

5 Droughts can have significant economic impacts. Explain **three** ways a prolonged drought might affect a farming community.

1 ....

2 ....

3 ....

Predict

6 Imagine you are the leader the council of a small town experiencing frequent droughts. What **three** water conservation measures would you implement?

1 ....

....

2 ....

....

3 ....

....

7 How do you think advances in technology might help us predict and manage droughts better in the next 20 years?

....

....

....

....

2.6 In what ways can drought management strategies mitigate climate change?

Revisit

1 Think about what you have learned about the relationship between vegetation and climate. How might drought management strategies that focus on preserving plant life help combat climate change?

....
....
....
....

2 Recall what you know about the carbon cycle. How could efficient water use in agriculture potentially reduce greenhouse gas emissions?

....
....

Expand

3 Drought-resistant crops are one strategy for managing droughts. Explain how using these crops might also help in reducing climate change impacts.

....
....
....

4 Describe **three** ways that improving irrigation systems could both manage drought and potentially mitigate climate change.

1 ....

2 ....

3 ....

2.6 Chapter 2 How might climate change affect drainage basins?

Predict

5 Imagine you are designing a drought management plan for a large city. What **three** strategies would you include that could also help reduce the city's carbon footprint?

1 ....
....

2 ....
....

3 ....
....

6 How do you think drought management strategies might evolve over the next 30 years to better address both water scarcity and climate change?

....
....
....
....
....
....

2.7 What is salination and how is it affected by climate change?

Revisit

1 Think about what you have learned about the water cycle. How might increased evaporation due to climate change lead to higher salination in water bodies?

....

....

....

....

2 Recall what you know about sea level rise. How could this contribute to increased salination in coastal areas?

....

....

Expand

3 You have learned that salination can affect ecosystems. Describe **two** ways increased salinity might impact freshwater species.

1 ....

2 ....

4 Salination can have various effects on agriculture. Explain **three** ways increased soil salinity might impact crop production.

1 ....

2 ....

3 ....

2.7 Chapter 2 How might climate change affect drainage basins?

Predict

5 Imagine you are a scientist studying a coastal wetland. What **three** changes would you expect to see in the ecosystem if salination increases over the next 20 years?

1 ....

....

2 ....

....

3 ....

....

6 How do you think advances in desalination technology might help address water quality issues related to climate change in the future?

....

....

....

....

....

....

2.8 How can you use mapping and GIS to study drainage basins?

Revisit

1 Think about what you have learned about drainage basins. How might GIS help us better understand the shape and characteristics of a drainage basin?

....

....

....

....

2 Recall what you know about flood risk. How could mapping technology help identify areas most at risk of flooding?

....

....

Expand

3 GIS can be used to analyse land-use patterns. Explain how this information might be useful in managing water resources within a drainage basin.

....

....

....

4 Describe **three** ways that satellite imagery, as part of GIS, could help us monitor changes in drainage basins over time.

1 ....

2 ....

3 ....

2.8 Chapter 2 How might climate change affect drainage basins?

Predict

5 Imagine you are using GIS to plan for future water needs in your region. What **three** types of data would you collect and analyse to make informed decisions?

1 ....

....

2 ....

....

3 ....

....

6 How do you think advancements in GIS and mapping technologies might change the way we study and manage drainage basins in the next 25 years?

....

....

....

....

....

....

Chapter 3 — Why does the Lake District look different from the Himalayas?

3.1 How do landscapes form and change over time?

Revisit

1 Add the following labels to Figure 3.1:

Eurasian plate   Indian plate   Collision boundary   Fold mountains forming Himalayas

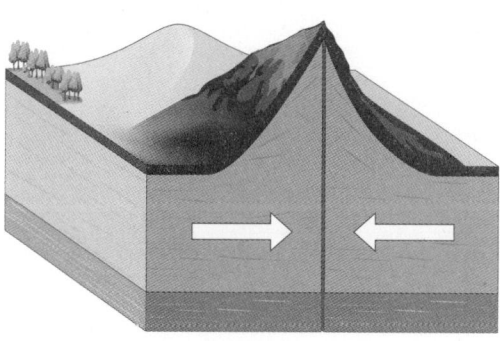

Figure 3.1

2 Remember what you learned about rocks. How might different types of rocks affect how quickly a landscape changes?

....

....

....

....

3 Think about what you know about weather. How could changes in temperature affect the way landscapes form?

....

....

....

Expand

4 You learned that both internal and external forces shape landscapes. Give **two** examples of how water can change a landscape over time.

   1 ....

   2 ....

3.1 Chapter 3 Why does the Lake District look different from the Himalayas?

5 Landscapes can change quickly or slowly. Describe **three** ways a volcanic eruption might change a landscape.

1 ....

2 ....

3 ....

Predict

6 Imagine you could travel one million years into the future. How might your local landscape look different? Explain why.

....

....

....

....

....

....

7 How do you think human activities might change landscapes in the next 100 years?

....

....

....

....

....

....

3.2 Chapter 3 Why does the Lake District look different from the Himalayas?

3.2 What are the main differences and similarities between the Lake District and the Himalayas?

Revisit

1 Think about what you have learned about mountains. How might the age of mountains affect their appearance?

....

....

....

....

2 Recall what you know about climate. How might the climate in the Lake District differ from that in the Himalayas?

....

....

Expand

3 You have learned that both areas are popular with tourists. Give **two** reasons why people might want to visit the Lake District.

1 ....

2 ....

4 Both regions face environmental challenges. Describe **three** ways tourism might affect these landscapes.

1 ....

2 ....

3 ....

Chapter 3 Why does the Lake District look different from the Himalayas?

5 Using the Venn diagram in Figure 3.2, list similarities and differences between the physical and environmental characteristics of the Lake District and the Himalayas.

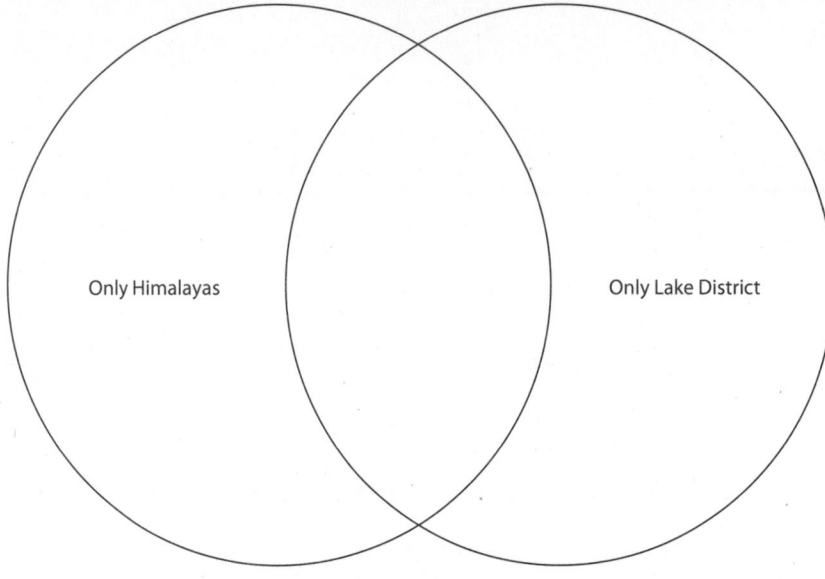

Figure 3.2

Predict

6 Imagine climate change causes temperatures to rise by 2 °C in both regions. How might this affect the Lake District and the Himalayas differently?

....

....

....

....

7 How do you think technology might change the way people explore these landscapes in the future?

....

....

....

....

3.3 Chapter 3 Why does the Lake District look different from the Himalayas?

3.3 How do climate and geography influence the plants and animals in each region?

Revisit

1 Remember what you learned about adaptations. How might animals in the Himalayas adapt to living at high altitudes?

....

....

....

2 Think about what you know about plant growth. How might the wet climate of the Lake District affect the types of plants that grow there?

....

....

Expand

3 Using your knowledge from question 1, add labels to Figure 3.3 to show the adaptations the Himalayan Yak has made to survive in the climate.

Figure 3.3 Himalayan Yak.

37

3.3 Chapter 3 Why does the Lake District look different from the Himalayas?

4 You learned that climate varies with altitude in the Himalayas. Give **two** examples of how plant life might change as you go up a mountain.

1 ....

2 ....

5 Both regions have unique ecosystems. Describe **three** ways animals might depend on plants in the Lake District.

1 ....

2 ....

3 ....

Predict

6 Imagine a new species of bird is introduced to the Lake District. How might this affect the existing ecosystem? Before answering this, think about what type of bird is being introduced.

....

....

....

....

....

7 How do you think climate change might affect the distribution of plants and animals in the Himalayas over the next 50 years?

....

....

....

....

....

3.4 Chapter 3 Why does the Lake District look different from the Himalayas?

3.4 How have humans adapted to live in these diverse landscapes?

Revisit

1 Think about what you have learned about farming. How might farming techniques in the Himalayas differ from those in flatter areas?

....

....

....

....

2 Recall what you know about building materials. How might houses in the Lake District be designed to cope with lots of rain?

....

....

Expand

3 You have learned that humans use local resources. Give **two** examples of how people in the Himalayas might use yaks in their daily lives.

1 ....

2 ....

4 Both regions have traditional ways of life. Describe **three** ways tourism might have changed life in the Lake District.

1 ....

2 ....

3 ....

3.4 Chapter 3 Why does the Lake District look different from the Himalayas?

Predict

5 Imagine new technology makes it easier to live in very cold places. How might this affect human settlements in the Himalayas?

....

....

....

....

....

....

6 How do you think traditional ways of life in these regions might change in the next 100 years?

....

....

....

....

....

....

Chapter 3 Why does the Lake District look different from the Himalayas?

3.5 What impact do human activities have on these environments?

Revisit

1 Think about what you have learned about ecosystems. How might deforestation in the Himalayas affect the plants and animals that live there?

....

....

....

....

2 Recall what you know about erosion. How could tourism in the Lake District contribute to soil erosion?

....

....

Expand

3 Human activities can affect mountain landscapes in both positive and negative ways. Complete Table 3.1 by adding one positive and one negative impact for each activity.

(For example: Tourism positive = jobs created for local people, Tourism negative = erosion of footpaths).

Cause (human activity)	Positive impact	Negative impact
Tourism		
Farming		
Deforestation		
Conservation		
Building roads		

Table 3.1

3.5 Chapter 3 Why does the Lake District look different from the Himalayas?

4 You have learned that human activities can have both positive and negative impacts. Give **two** examples of how conservation efforts might help protect these landscapes.

1 ....

2 ....

5 Climate change is affecting both regions. Describe **three** ways melting glaciers in the Himalayas might impact the environment and people living there.

1 ....

2 ....

3 ....

Predict

6 Imagine you are in charge of managing tourism in the Lake District. What **three** rules would you create to help protect the environment while still allowing visitors?

1 ....

2 ....

3 ....

7 How do you think sustainable practices in agriculture and tourism might change the Lake District's landscape over the next 50 years?

....

....

....

....

....

....

3.6 How do these landscapes influence culture and daily life?

Chapter 3 Why does the Lake District look different from the Himalayas?

Revisit

1 Think about what you have learned about art and literature. How has the Lake District inspired famous writers and painters?

....

....

....

....

2 Recall what you know about the geography of the Himalayas. How do the mountains influence the daily lives of people living in that region?

....

....

Expand

3 You have learned that landscapes can shape local traditions. Give **two** examples of how the natural environment in either region might influence festivals or community events.

1 ....

2 ....

4 Both regions have influenced how people see themselves. Describe **three** ways that living in a mountainous area might shape someone's identity or lifestyle.

1 ....

2 ....

3 ....

3.6 Chapter 3 Why does the Lake District look different from the Himalayas?

Predict

5 Imagine you grew up in the Lake District and then moved to a big city. How might your connection to nature change, and what **three** things might you miss most about the landscape?

1 ....
....

2 ....
....

3 ....
....

6 How do you think future generations living in the Himalayas might view their relationship with the mountains differently than people do today?

....
....
....
....
....

3.7 Chapter 3 Why does the Lake District look different from the Himalayas?

3.7 What environmental challenges do these regions face, and how are they being addressed?

Revisit

1. Add these three labels in the correct position on Figure 3.4:

   Melting   Retreat   U-shaped valley

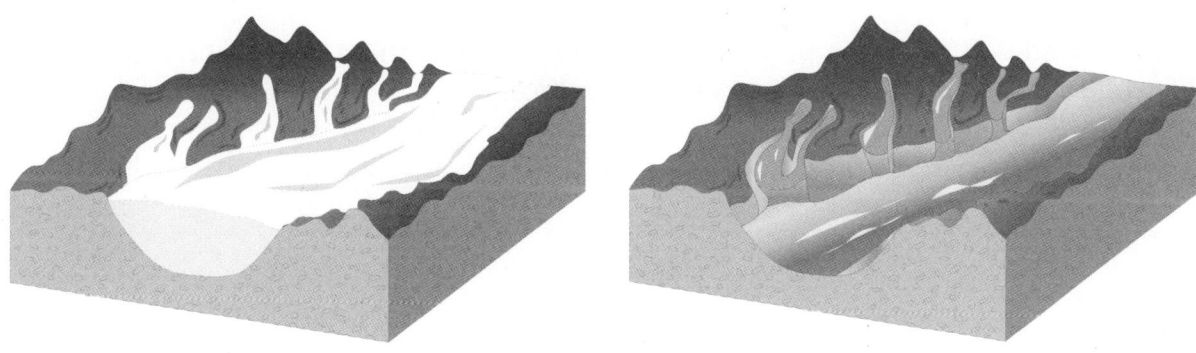

Figure 3.4

2. Think about what you have learned about climate change. How might rising temperatures affect the glaciers in the Himalayas?

   ....

   ....

   ....

   ....

3. Recall what you know about pollution. How could air pollution from cities impact the ecosystems in these mountain regions?

   ....

   ....

   ....

   ....

3.7 Chapter 3 Why does the Lake District look different from the Himalayas?

Expand

4 You have learned that both regions face challenges from tourism. Give **two** examples of how too many visitors might harm the environment in the Lake District.

1 ....

2 ....

5 Conservation efforts are important in both areas. Describe **three** ways that creating protected areas might help preserve these landscapes.

1 ....

2 ....

3 ....

Predict

6 Imagine you are a scientist studying the Lake District. What **three** changes do you think you might observe in the landscape over the next 100 years due to climate change?

1 ....

2 ....

3 ....

7 How do you think new technologies might be used to address environmental challenges in the Himalayas in the future?

....

....

....

....

....

3.8 How can we appreciate and preserve diverse landscapes around the world?

Revisit

1 Think about what you have learned about ecosystems. Why is it important to preserve diverse landscapes for maintaining Earth's biodiversity?

....

....

....

....

2 Recall what you know about responsible tourism. How can following 'Leave No Trace' principles help protect natural areas?

....

....

Expand

3 You have learned that education is important for preservation. Give **two** ways that learning about different landscapes can help protect them.

1 ....

2 ....

4 Local communities play a role in conservation. Describe **three** ways that people living near these landscapes can help preserve them.

1 ....

2 ....

3 ....

3.8 Chapter 3 Why does the Lake District look different from the Himalayas?

5 Choosing one of the Lake District, the Himalayas or your local environment, design a poster in the frame below encouraging people to protect the landscape. (You may wish to use the 'leave no trace' principles to help you.)

Predict

6 Imagine you are creating a new social media app to help people appreciate landscapes. What **three** features would you include to encourage responsible sharing and protection of natural areas?

1 ....

....

2 ....

....

3 ....

....

Chapter 4 How does life adapt to its environment?

4.1 How does climate affect the world's biomes?

Connect back

1 Why is the average temperature hot in Kerala throughout the year?

....

....

....

2 Describe the climate of your location. How does it compare with Kerala and Rajasthan?

....

....

....

Expand

3 Annotate Figure 4.1 to explain how the climate is affecting the changes in vegetation.

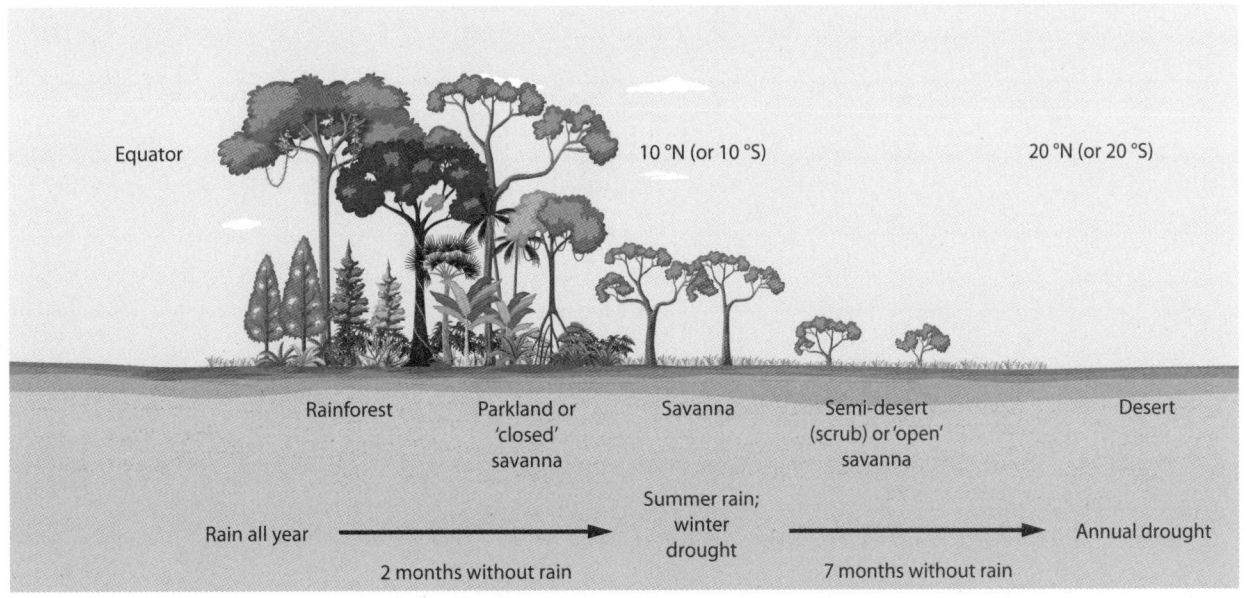

Figure 4.1 A diagram showing how vegetation changes from rainforest to desert.

4.1 Chapter 4 How does life adapt to its environment?

4 Why do biomes change slowly from rainforest to desert?

....

....

....

....

Predict

5 What challenges do you think the climate of Rajasthan might create for people?

....

....

....

....

....

6 Do you think the climate of Rajasthan, Kerala or your location will create more opportunities for people? Explain your answer.

....

....

....

....

....

....

....

....

4.2 What are the characteristics of hot desert biomes?

Connect back

1. Draw a picture of an animal found in a hot desert environment. Annotate it to show how the creature has adapted to the conditions found there.

2. Figure 4.2 shows a desert landscape. Annotate it to explain why it looks the way that it does.

Figure 4.2 A desert landscape.

Expand

3. Describe the climate in your local environment. Remember to describe how temperature and precipitation vary over the year.

....

....

....

....

4.2 Chapter 4 How does life adapt to its environment?

4 Explain how plants and animals have adapted to conditions in your local environment.

....

....

....

....

....

Predict

5 What do you think would happen if there was an increase in precipitation in hot deserts? How would this change the landscape, the plants and the animals that are currently found there?

....

....

....

....

....

....

6 How might people have to adapt to living in hot deserts like the Thar Desert? What challenges would they have to overcome?

....

....

....

....

....

4.3 How do people adapt to life in hot deserts?

Connect back

1 State **three** challenges with living in hot deserts.

1 ....

2 ....

3 ....

2 Explain how modern innovations are helping people to overcome these challenges.

....

....

....

....

Expand

3 Figure 4.3 shows Khadeens in place in the desert. Annotate the diagram to explain how these low stone walls help farmers in hot deserts.

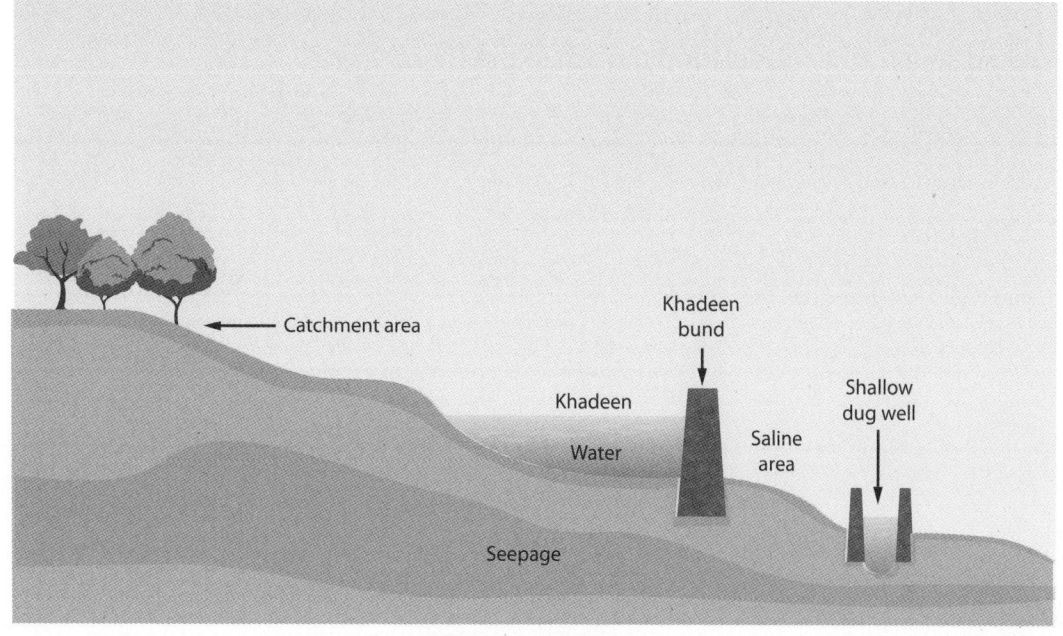

Figure 4.3 Khadeens.

4.3
Chapter 4 How does life adapt to its environment?

4 The term 'appropriate technology' is used to describe technology that meets local needs, and uses local materials and local knowledge and skills.

Why would Khadeens be classed as appropriate technology?

....

....

....

....

Predict

5 The Thar Desert is the most densely populated desert in the world. Why might so many people be able to live in such an extreme environment?

....

....

....

....

6 What could limit further population growth in the Thar Desert?

....

....

....

....

4.4 What are the opportunities for people in hot deserts?

Connect back

1 This is a conflict matrix. Complete it by writing in how each group might conflict with another. An example has been done for you.

	Farmers	Miners	Tourists	Locals
Farmers		Remove land for grazing animals		
Miners				
Tourists				
Locals				

2 Which form of development do you think will cause the most conflict? Explain your answer.

....

....

....

Expand

3 What opportunities for development are there in your local environment? How does the physical geography of the place you live in affect these opportunities?

....

....

4.4 Chapter 4 How does life adapt to its environment?

4 What conflict arises from developments in your local environment?

....

....

....

....

....

Predict

5 How might climate change affect the challenges and opportunities of living in a hot desert environment?

....

....

....

....

....

....

....

....

6 How might people have to adapt to a changing climate in hot deserts?

....

....

....

....

4.5 What are the characteristics of cold desert biomes?

Connect back

1 Figure 4.4 shows the precipitation for Utqiagvik in northern Alaska. Add the temperature data to the graph.

Month	Temperature (°C)
Jan	−21
Feb	−21
Mar	−20
Apr	−13
May	−3
Jun	5
Jul	8
Aug	7
Sep	3
Oct	−5
Nov	−13
Dec	−18

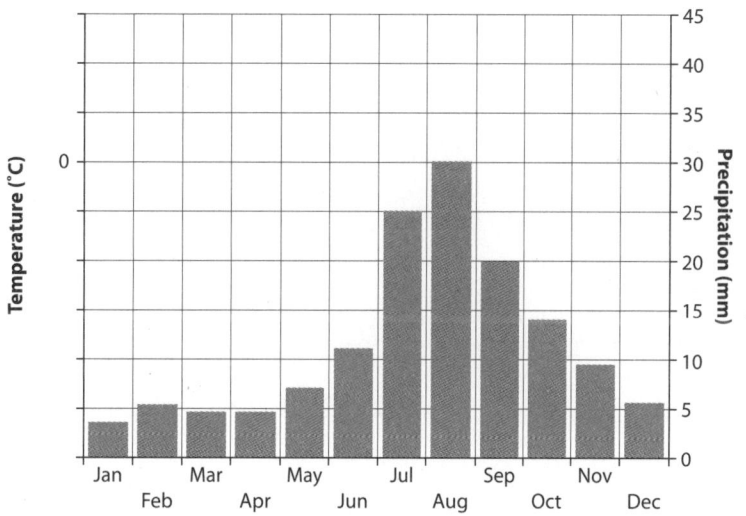

Figure 4.4 A climate graph for Utqiagvik, Alaska.

2 Utqiagvik is in the Arctic Circle. Explain why the temperature is so cold in winter but warmer in summer.

....

....

....

....

Expand

3 Permafrost is permanently frozen soil. On a separate piece of paper, draw a spider diagram showing the impact that permafrost will have on animals, plants and people.

4.5 Chapter 4 How does life adapt to its environment?

4 What are the similarities between the landscapes of hot and cold deserts?

....

....

....

....

Predict

5 How will climate change affect the cold desert environment? Consider plants, animals and the landscape.

....

....

....

....

....

6 People living in cold desert environments will face challenges. Which challenges do you think will be similar to those living in hot deserts and which will be different?

....

....

....

....

....

4.6 How do people adapt to life in cold deserts?

Connect back

1 Make a list of all the challenges faced by people in cold deserts. Rank them from the most significant to the least.

....

....

2 Do the same for the challenges faced by hot desert environments. See how many you can remember without looking back in the Student's Book or your own notes.

....

....

Expand

3 Draw a diagram of a house in a cold desert. Annotate it to explain how it has been adapted to meet the conditions found there.

4.6 Chapter 4 How does life adapt to its environment?

4 How are houses different in your local environment? Add further annotation to your diagram to explain.

Predict

5 Population density in cold deserts is usually very low. What do you think would happen if it increased?

....

....

....

....

....

6 Is the population more likely to grow in hot or cold deserts? Explain your rationale.

....

....

....

....

....

4.7 What are the opportunities for people in cold deserts?

Connect back

1 How might indigenous people be affected by increased development in cold deserts?

....

....

....

2 What are the similarities and differences in the opportunities found in cold and hot deserts?

....

....

....

....

Expand

This map shows population density in Russia.

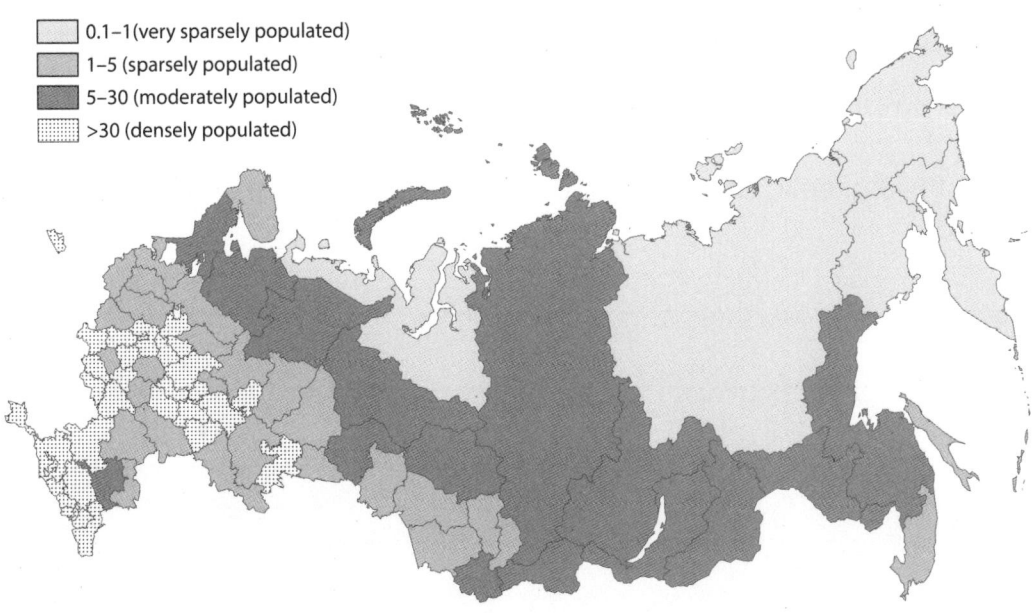

Figure 4.5 A map showing population density in Russia.

3 Describe the distribution of people in Russia.

....

....

....

4 Explain the challenges created by having a sparse population.

....

....

....

....

Predict

5 Why might we need a Global Seed Vault? What could happen in the future to mean that it was necessary?

....

....

....

....

6 Why might the economic activity in cold desert regions increase the need for a Global Seed Vault?

....

....

....

....

4.8 What does the future hold for people living in extreme environments?

Connect back

1 Some people might assume that global warming will make life easier in cold deserts. Why is this not the case?

....

....

....

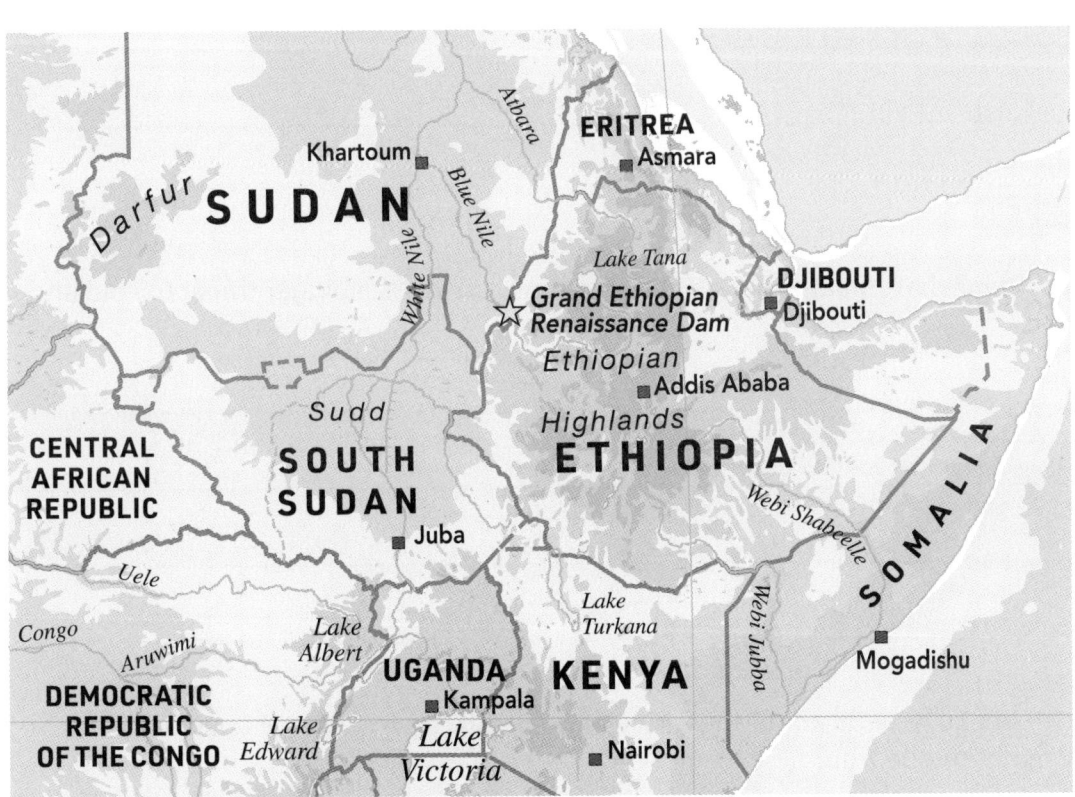

Figure 4.6 The location of Grand Ethiopian Renaissance Dam.

2 Describe the location of the Grand Ethiopian Renaissance Dam (GERD) and explain why climate change makes it more likely that its construction will cause conflict.

....

....

....

4.8 Chapter 4 How does life adapt to its environment?

Expand

3 How might climate change affect your local environment?

....

....

....

4 How might people be affected by these changes?

....

....

....

Predict

5 Do you think that climate change or population growth is a bigger threat to cold and hot deserts?

....

....

....

....

6 'We should be hopeful about the future of people living in extreme environments.' Why might this be true?

....

....

....

....

Chapter 5 What can be done to ensure everyone has enough food?

5.1 Is global food production keeping up with population growth?

Connect back

1 What milestone in global population was passed in 2022?

....

....

....

2 a How has the world's population grown since 1800 compared with before 1800?

....

....

b Has food production kept pace with this growth? Explain your answer.

....

....

....

Expand

3 Suggest **three** innovations which have allowed food production to increase dramatically since the 1950s.

1 ....

....

2 ....

....

3 ....

....

65

Chapter 5 What can be done to ensure everyone has enough food?

4 What **four** factors are used to calculate the Global Food Security Index (GFSI) score for each country?

1 ....

2 ....

3 ....

4 ....

Predict

5 For one of the challenges in Figure 5.1, suggest how it will potentially affect future crop yields.

....

....

....

....

....

....

....

....

Figure 5.1 Potential challenges which will affect future food supply.

Factors affecting future crop yields:
- Global soil fertility is declining
- Global soil moisture levels are decreasing
- Droughts are more common
- Global temperatures are rising
- Conflict and political tensions
- Uncertainties in the global food chain

....

....

....

....

5.1   **Chapter 5 What can be done to ensure everyone has enough food?**

6 Figure 5.2 shows a palm oil plantation with palm fruits.

Figure 5.2 Palm oil is used in many ultra-processed foods, on land that used to be tropical forests.

How does the large-scale production of this crop impact the environment and people's health?

....

....

....

....

....

5.2 What is food security and why does it vary?

Connect back

1 Which country produces the most agricultural products by value?

....

....

2 Suggest **two** water-related problems that farmers face, which might affect food production.

1 ....

....

2 ....

....

Expand

3 For one of the countries listed here, suggest **two** reasons why their food security score is so low.

Best performers	Food security score
Finland	83.7
Ireland	81.7
Norway	80.5
France	80.2
Netherlands	80.1

Weakest performers	Food security score
Syria	36.3
Haiti	38.5
Yemen	40.1
Sierra Leone	40.5
Madagascar	40.6

Table 5.1 Countries with the highest and lowest Global Food Security Index scores in 2022.

1 ....

....

2 ....

....

5.2 Chapter 5 What can be done to ensure everyone has enough food?

Predict

4 The lesson title asks how food security varies. How does (or might) it vary:

  a globally?

  ....

  ....

  b within your own country?

  ....

  ....

  c over time?

  ....

  ....

5 For each of the factors below, add some more detail to explain why it might reduce the level of food security.

  a new solar farms

  ....

  ....

  b dependence on food imports from overseas

  ....

  ....

  c overuse of chemicals by farmers

  ....

  ....

5.3 Why is soil so important?

Connect back

1 Define the term food security.

....

....

2 On what percentage of the Earth's land area is the soil good enough for food production?

....

Expand

3 What are the **four** elements that make up a soil?

1 ....

2 ....

3 ....

4 ....

4 How can the relative proportions of these **four** elements change the quality of a soil for food production?

1 ....

2 ....

3 ....

4 ....

5.3 Chapter 5 What can be done to ensure everyone has enough food?

Predict

5 Soil texture is shown on a pyramid graph (Figure 5.3). This shows changes to three variables on one diagram. They can be slightly tricky to interpret.

Look at the example below. The cross shows a clay soil. To find the percentages of sand, silt and clay you:

- Read up the left-hand axis for clay, using the horizontal lines parallel to the base of the pyramid – this gives a reading of 50 per cent clay.
- Next, read up the right-hand axis, using the vertical lines parallel to the left-hand edge of the pyramid – this gives a reading of 20 per cent silt.
- Finally, read along the bottom axis, using the vertical lines parallel to the right-hand edge of the pyramid – this gives a reading of 30 per cent sand.

What percentage of each texture type does the soil marked by a circle have, which is classed as a silt loam?

Sand ....

Silt ....

Clay ....

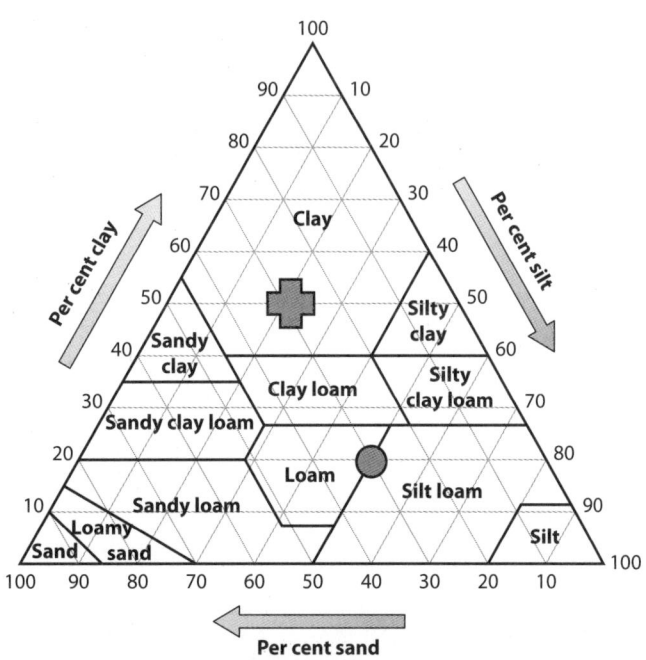

Figure 5.3 The soil texture pyramid.

6 What is the minimum percentage of clay that a clay soil can have?

....

5.4 How are the world's soils changing?

Connect back

1 What is regolith and how is it different from soil?

....

....

2 Why are earthworms important to soil formation?

....

....

Expand

3 Soils are negatively affected by **three** main processes which reduce their fertility. What are they?

1 ....

2 ....

3 ....

4 For **one** of the processes, outline some of the strategies being used to reduce the impacts.

....

....

....

....

....

5.4 Chapter 5 What can be done to ensure everyone has enough food?

Predict

5 What are the positive impacts of volcanic activity on the soils across Indonesia?

....

....

....

....

6 Investigate the work Justdiggit does across Africa using their website. Write a summary of some of their achievements.

....

....

....

....

....

....

....

....

....

....

....

....

....

Chapter 5 What can be done to ensure everyone has enough food?

5.5 How does the global food supply system work?

Connect back

1 What percentage of the world's food is grown in soil?

....

2 Fill in the gaps in the paragraph below using words from the word bank:

> conflict   consumption   produced   resilience   supply   sea

The global food .... system (GFSS) is a web of activities involving the production, processing, transport and .... of food. Food is .... in many parts of the world and transported to areas where people live by land, ... or air. The system needs to build .... to shocks, which include climate change and international ....

Expand

3 Figure 5.4 shows the journey of a bag of carrots. Carrots are grown and harvested on a farm near Boston, England. The packing and processing factory is near Spalding, where the carrots are washed, checked and packaged in plastic bags.

The carrots are sent to a supermarket warehouse near Peterborough to be kept in cold conditions, before being sent to the supermarket in Ely where a customer buys them and takes them two miles home before they are eaten.

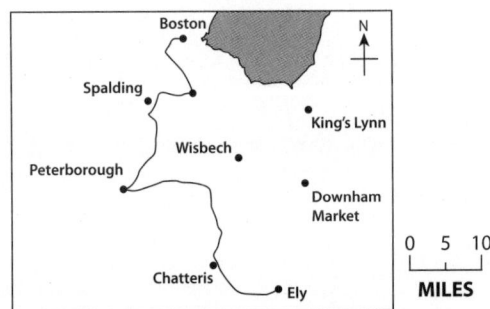

Figure 5.4 The journey of a bag of carrots.

a Use the map and the scale on the map to work out the total food miles travelled by the carrots.

Starting point	End point	Miles travelled
1: The farm near Boston	2: The factory near Spalding	
2: The factory near Spalding	3: The supermarket warehouse near Peterborough	
3: The supermarket warehouse near Peterborough	4: The supermarket in Ely	
4: The supermarket in Ely	Home	
	Total food miles	

5.5 Chapter 5 What can be done to ensure everyone has enough food?

b How far is it from the farm to Ely in a straight line? ....

4 Why does a higher amount of food miles not necessarily mean that food has a greater environmental impact than food that has only travelled a short distance?

....

....

Predict

5 How does Aotearoa New Zealand benefit from being part of the global food supply system?

....

....

....

6 Read the newspaper story below, which was from June 2025.

> **New Zealanders' anger as butter price rises**
>
> Dairy products like milk and butter are New Zealand's largest export industry, but butter prices have risen by 65 per cent in a year. Some people are driving long distances to find cheap butter or ordering it from Australia where it is cheaper. Some people have started making their own butter. New Zealand produces a third of all the world's dairy trade. Supply problems and high demand have meant butter prices have risen, and it is the price paid in other countries that determines the price that people in New Zealand have to pay. So while the economy benefits, individual people end up paying more.

Why is Aotearoa New Zealand's involvement in exporting food globally creating a problem for its population?

....

....

....

....

5.5 Chapter 5 What can be done to ensure everyone has enough food?

7 Visit the Marine Traffic website and zoom out to a world view. Container ships are shown by large green arrows.

On Figure 5.5, plot the obvious routes that you can see them taking between ports in China and Singapore and those in Europe and the USA.

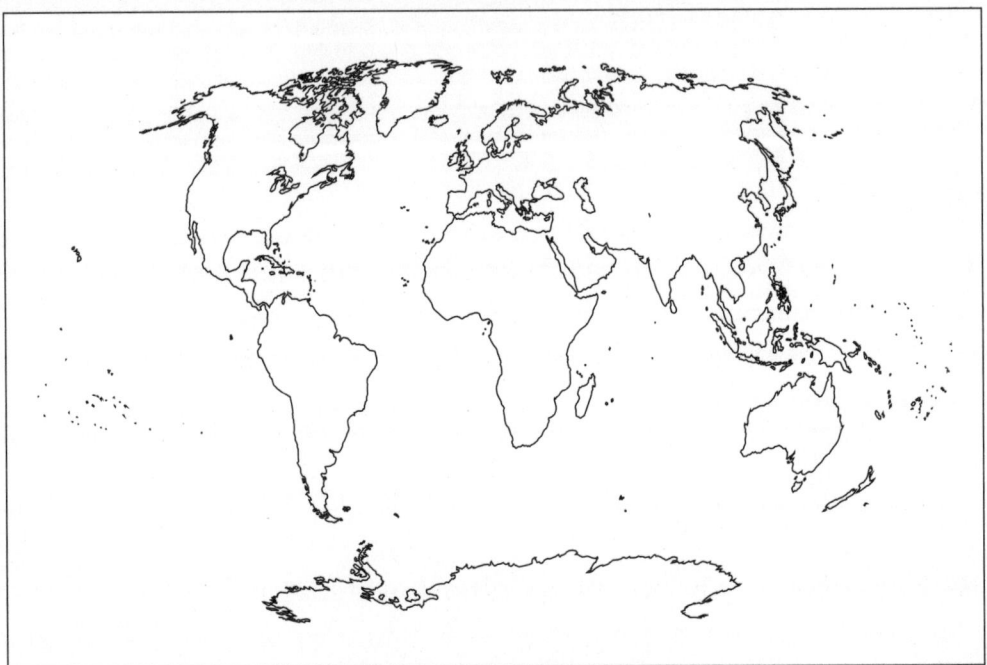

Figure 5.5 A map of the world.

5.6 How can a country improve its food security?

Connect back

1 Define the term food miles.

....

....

2 What are *konbini* and why are they a popular choice for urban residents in Japan to source their food?

....

....

3 List the foods that you have eaten so far today that you think were probably produced outside of your home country. How might these foods have reached you?

....

....

....

Expand

4 What environmental issues are created in the Almeria area of southern Spain, shown in Figure 5.6?

....

....

....

....

Figure 5.6 Almeria in southern Spain.

....

....

5.6 Chapter 5 What can be done to ensure everyone has enough food?

5 The global food supply system's resilience to shocks has been tested in recent years. Suggest at least **two** events which might have caused disruption.

....

....

....

Predict

In the UK, one way to support food security in vulnerable groups is the work of the Trussell Trust and other charities who run food banks.

6 Table 5.2 shows the number of food parcels distributed in England. Draw a line graph of the data in the framework provided.

Year	Food parcels (millions)
2017–18	1
2018–19	1.2
2019–20	1.5
2020–21	2.1
2021–22	1.8
2022–23	2.5
2023–24	2.6

Table 5.2

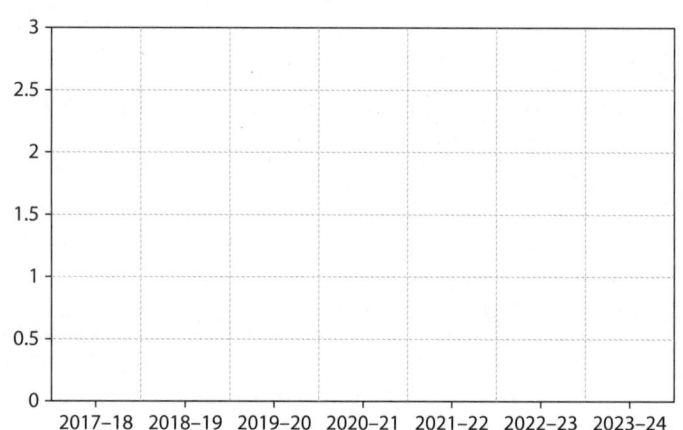

7 Describe the general trend in the number of food parcels distributed between 2017 and 2024.

....

....

....

8 Can you suggest which event caused food bank usage to drop in 2021–22?

....

5.7 Why does it matter what people choose to eat?

Connect back

1. Suggest **two** ways that governments can improve the food security of the country they oversee.

   1 ....

   2 ....

2. What problems may result from increasing food insecurity caused by rising food prices?

   ....

   ....

   ....

   ....

Expand

3. Outline some of the environmental problems that are created by the growing of avocados in South America for export around the world.

   ....

   ....

   ....

   ....

4. What steps is the government of Finland taking to ensure that its food security remains high?

   ....

   ....

   ....

   ....

5.7 Chapter 5 What can be done to ensure everyone has enough food?

Predict

5 This person is shopping in a supermarket in a high-income country (HIC). Design a flyer which could be placed in each shopping basket to suggest why shoppers might want to choose more vegetarian options.

Figure 5.7 Shoppers in many HICs source much of their food from supermarkets, whose decisions influence the diet of many customers.

6 Suggest **three** reasons why people outside of low-income countries (LICs) might choose to eat insect protein as part of their diet.

1 ....

2 ....

3 ....

7 Suggest **three** ways that food waste could be reduced in your own home area.

1 ....

2 ....

3 ....

5.8 What impact might climate change have on future food production?

Connect back

1 Why does eating a plant-based diet have less impact on the environment?

....

....

....

2 What are ultra-processed foods? Give some examples of them.

....

....

....

Expand

3 Look at the newspaper headlines below. How is climate change affecting farmers, and the resources they need to continue producing food?

> Farmers hoping for an end to the dry spell
>
> Farmers worried about delays in harvesting due to prolonged rain
>
> Hailstorm causes damage to the maize crop
>
> Farmers face restrictions on water extraction from rivers
>
> Cocoa prices rise to record levels following extreme heat in Ghana

....

....

....

5.8 Chapter 5 What can be done to ensure everyone has enough food?

4 Around half of the world's habitable land area is used for agriculture. How could this area be increased?

....

....

....

Predict

5 a Look at Figure 5.8. Which parts of the world have the highest rates of food waste?

....

b What percentage of food is thrown away in North America?

....

c What percentage of food is thrown away in the Middle East and North Africa region?

....

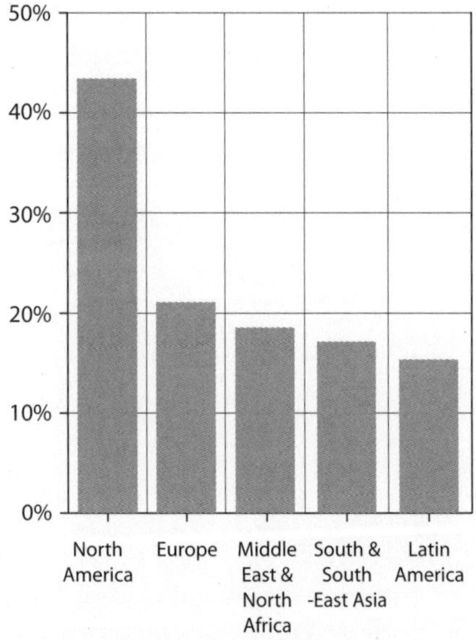

Figure 5.8 Percentage of food calories lost and wasted during the production process.

d Why do you think that levels of food waste are lower in LICs than in HICs?

....

....

6 Suggest at least **two** ways that farmers might prepare their farms to be more resilient to the impacts of climate change.

1 ....

....

2 ....

....

Chapter 6: What impacts will a changing climate have?

6.1 How can we classify the impacts of climate change?

Connect back

1 State **two** ways in which we can classify impacts.

1 ....

2 ....

2 Why is it important to classify impacts?

....

....

Expand

3 Explain the three different types of impact in your own words. Give at least one example of each.

Environmental

....

....

Social

....

....

Economic

....

....

6.1 Chapter 6 What impacts will a changing climate have?

Predict

4 Which type of impacts – environmental, social or economic – do you think are likely to have the greatest impact on you as an individual? Why do you think this?

....

....

....

....

....

....

....

5 Do you think the impacts of climate change are likely to become better or worse over time? Why do you think this?

....

....

....

....

....

....

....

....

....

6.2 What is the health of the planet?

Connect back

1 Why is it important to look at planetary health rather than just climate change?

....

....

....

2 Which of the following is the odd one out? Why?

        land use   ozone   climate change   pollution

....

....

Expand

3 Explain a feedback loop associated with climate change.

....

....

....

....

4 How would you explain the idea of a tipping point to a friend?

....

....

....

....

6.2

Chapter 6 What impacts will a changing climate have?

Predict

5 If the Atlantic Ocean current warmed beyond its tipping point, what might be some of the impacts of this? (Think back to Chapter 1 to help you.)

....

....

....

....

....

....

6 'If the hole in the ozone layer can be reversed, there is hope for fixing some of the other indicators of planetary health.' To what extent do you agree with this statement?

....

....

....

....

....

....

....

....

6.3 What are some environmental impacts of climate change?

Connect back

1 What is the definition of an extreme weather event?

....

....

2 Why might sea-level rise be a problem?

....

....

Expand

3 Carry out some research using a newspaper or the internet into an extreme weather event that has happened this year.

Chapter 6 What impacts will a changing climate have?

4 To what extent do you think that this extreme weather event was made more severe by climate change? Explain your answer.

....

....

....

....

....

Predict

5 Which communities do you think will be most affected by extreme weather events and sea-level rise? Why do you think this?

....

....

....

....

....

6 How do you think governments should respond to these environmental impacts? Why?

....

....

....

....

....

6.4 More environmental impacts of climate change

Connect back

1 Can you think of a way to remember the four main environmental impacts of climate change that you have explored in this and the previous lesson?

....

....

....

2 Use an atlas to find the locations of the following coral reefs: Great Barrier Reef, Mesoamerican Barrier Reef, New Caledonia Barrier Reef, Red Sea Coral Reef and Florida Reef. Mark them on the world map in Figure 6.1.

Figure 6.1 Map of the world.

6.4 Chapter 6 What impacts will a changing climate have?

Expand

3 Coral reef bleaching happens locally but can have global impacts. What might some of these global impacts be?

....

....

....

4 Describe what being in a mangrove forest is like. What can you hear, see, touch, smell? Why?

....

....

....

Predict

5 Why do you think that coral reefs are popular tourist destinations? What could happen to the tourism market if coral bleaching occurred?

....

....

....

6 If you were to order the **four** main environmental impacts of climate change from biggest impact to smallest impact, how would you order them and why?

Smallest impact ←—————————————————————————————→ Biggest impact

....

....

....

6.5 What are some economic impacts of climate change?

Connect back

1 What is GDP? Why is it important to know what this is in this particular lesson?

....

....

2 If crop yields reduce as a result of climate change, what is likely to happen? Complete the 'chain of reasoning' diagram in Figure 6.2 to show the knock-on effects. Make sure you use your knowledge from Chapter 5 too.

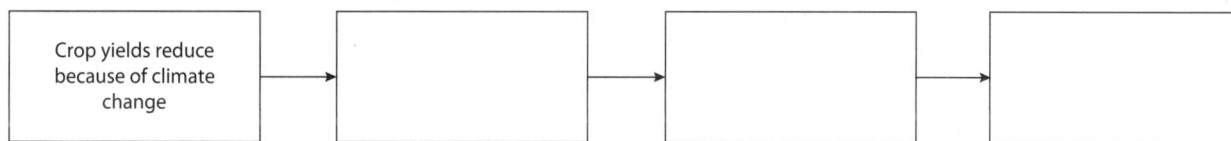

Figure 6.2

Expand

3 In Niger, 41.8 per cent of GDP is from agriculture. In Pakistan, the figure is 23.3 per cent and in Argentina it is 5.9 per cent. Which country do you think will be most affected economically by climate change? How might it be affected?

....

....

....

....

4 Agriculture is possibly the only area where some of the impacts of climate change could be positive. Do you think that the positives outweigh the negatives? Why do you think this?

....

....

....

....

6.5 Chapter 6 What impacts will a changing climate have?

Predict

5 Think about the last holiday you went on, or one that you would like to go on. Describe it and suggest how it might be affected by the impacts of climate change.

....

....

....

....

....

....

6 Many LICs, including the Maldives, are investing in tourism in order to develop their economy. If you were an advisor to the Maldives, what threats to tourism would you identify and what would you suggest as a solution?

....

....

....

....

....

....

....

6.6 What are some of the social impacts of climate change?

Connect back

1 What are the **three** main ways that climate change can impact health?

1 ....

2 ....

3 ....

2 What does 'vulnerable' mean? Suggest some groups that are more vulnerable to the impacts of climate change.

....

....

....

....

Expand

3 Carry out some research in a book or on the internet about how climate change is impacting the spread of malaria. In particular, focus on those areas that are likely to now experience conditions suitable for malaria to spread, which did not before.

4 Physical and mental illness can have knock-on economic impacts. If someone is suffering from these social impacts of climate change, what might some of the economic impacts be?

....

....

....

6.6

Predict

5 Imagine that you are the leader of a region which has seen a significant increase in health issues as a result of climate change. What would you do to improve the lives of the people living in your region?

....

....

....

....

....

....

6 'Social impacts of climate change are likely to have the greatest impact on me as an individual.' To what extent do you agree with this statement?

....

....

....

....

....

....

6.7 What are climate refugees?

Connect back

1 What is a climate refugee?

....

....

2 Which parts of the world are likely to have the greatest number of climate refugees?

....

....

Expand

3 Explain what an NGO is. Can you give some examples of NGOs that might help climate refugees?

....

....

....

4 Why is the role of NGOs important in supporting climate refugees?

....

....

....

....

6.7 Chapter 6 What impacts will a changing climate have?

Predict

5 Read the graphic novel 'Everyday stories of climate change' by Gemma Sou (you can search for this in a search engine and download the comic in English, Spanish or Hindi). How does climate change impact the everyday life of families?

....

....

....

....

....

....

6 Create your own climate refugee graphic novel or comic to illustrate some of the issues facing people who are displaced as a result of climate change.

6.8 How will climate change impact Russia?

Connect back

1 What is permafrost? Why is its melting such a problem?

....

....

....

....

2 Use an atlas to locate the Northern Sea Route. Describe its location.

....

....

....

Expand

3 Why is Russia home to so many diverse environments?

HINT: Try to link your answer back to your learning from Chapter 1 and Chapter 4.

....

....

....

....

4 How might agriculture in Russia be impacted by climate change?

....

....

....

....

6.8 Chapter 6 What impacts will a changing climate have?

Predict

5 It is 2050. Use your knowledge from this lesson to write a story opener to describe what life is like living in Siberian Russia.

....

....

....

....

....

....

....

....

6 How might the impacts of climate change in Russia create more inequality in the country?

....

....

....

....

....

....